ELEPHANT

Dylanna Press

Copyright © 2025 by Dylanna Press
Author: Tyler Grady

All rights reserved. No part of this publication may be reproduced, stored in a retrieval system, or transmitted by any means, including electronic, mechanical, photocopying, or otherwise, without prior written permission of the publisher.

Although the publisher has taken all reasonable care in the preparation of this book, we make no warranty about the accuracy or completeness of its content and, to the maximum extent permitted, disclaim all liability arising from its use.

Trademarks: Dylanna Press is a registered trademark of Dylanna Publishing, Inc. and may not be used without written permission.

ISBN: 978-1647904289(pb); 978-1647904555 (hc)
Publisher: Dylanna Publishing, Inc.
First Edition: 2026

10 9 8 7 6 5 4 3 2 1

For information about special discounts for bulk purchases, please contact:
orders@dylannapublishing.com
Dylanna Publishing, Inc.
www.dylannapublishing.com

Contents

Meet the Elephant Family   7
Built for Greatness   8
Life in Many Lands   11
Super Survivors: Elephant Adaptations   12
What Do Elephants Eat?   15
Life in the Herd   16
On the Move   18
A Day in the Life   20
Mating and Birth   23
Growing Up Elephant   24
Elephants and Their Ecosystem   27
Natural Predators   28
Challenges and Threats   31
Life Span and Population   32
Future for Elephants   35
Test Your Elephant Knowledge!   36
STEM Challenge: Think Like a Scientist!   37
Word Search   38
Glossary   39
Resources and References   40
Index   41

Meet the Elephant Family

BRRRRUMMM! The ground trembles beneath your feet. A deep rumbling sound rolls across the African savanna—so low you feel it vibrate in your chest before you even hear it. Through the golden grass, a massive gray shape emerges: wrinkled skin, enormous fan-shaped ears, and two gleaming ivory tusks. Welcome to the world of elephants!

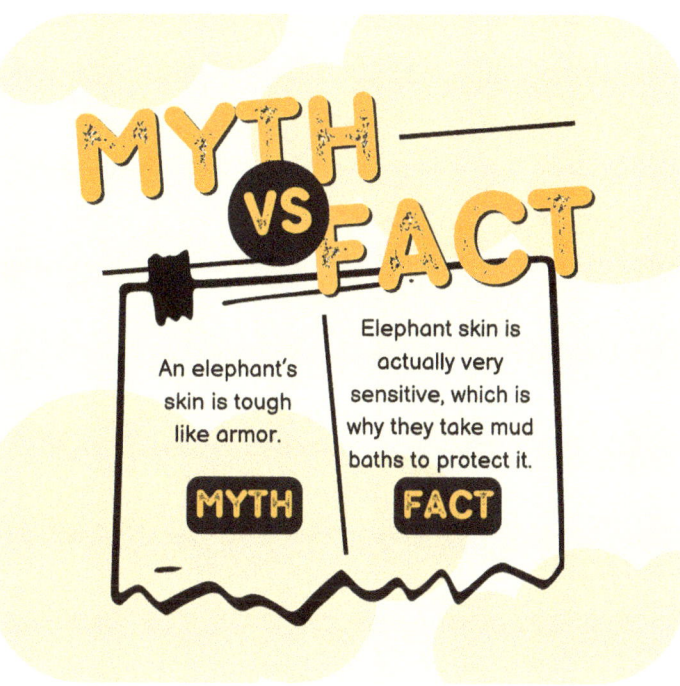

These magnificent giants are the largest land animals on Earth, roaming across Africa and Asia in thick forests and wide-open grasslands. Long ago, elephants wandered across huge stretches of territory, but today wild elephants are found mainly in protected areas across Africa and in fragmented reserves throughout Asia.

There are three elephant species alive today. African savanna elephants are the largest, with huge fan-shaped ears and long tusks. African forest elephants are smaller and darker, with oval-shaped ears and straighter tusks. Asian elephants are the smallest of the three, with smaller rounded ears—and only some males grow tusks. Their scientific family name is Elephantidae, and they are the only living members of this ancient family.

What makes elephants truly special? They're incredibly intelligent, deeply emotional, and fiercely loyal to their families. They remember faces for decades, mourn their dead, and communicate using sounds too low for human ears to hear.

For thousands of years, elephants have amazed people and played important roles in cultures around the world. As one of Earth's most intelligent and social animals, elephants continue to fascinate scientists with their complex behaviors and unbreakable family bonds.

Built for Greatness

It's hard to miss an elephant! These massive animals are the biggest land creatures on Earth and have some of the most unique features in the animal kingdom. African savanna elephants are the largest land animals alive today—an adult stands about 10 to 13 feet (3 to 4 meters) tall at the shoulder, about as tall as a one-story house! They can weigh between 6,000 to 12,000 pounds (2,700 to 5,400 kg), with males being significantly larger than females.

One of the elephant's most powerful features is its trunk. This long, muscular extension of its nose and upper lip is strong enough to lift heavy branches yet delicate enough to pick up a single peanut. Elephants use their trunks for just about everything—grabbing food, drinking water, smelling, communicating, and even playing!

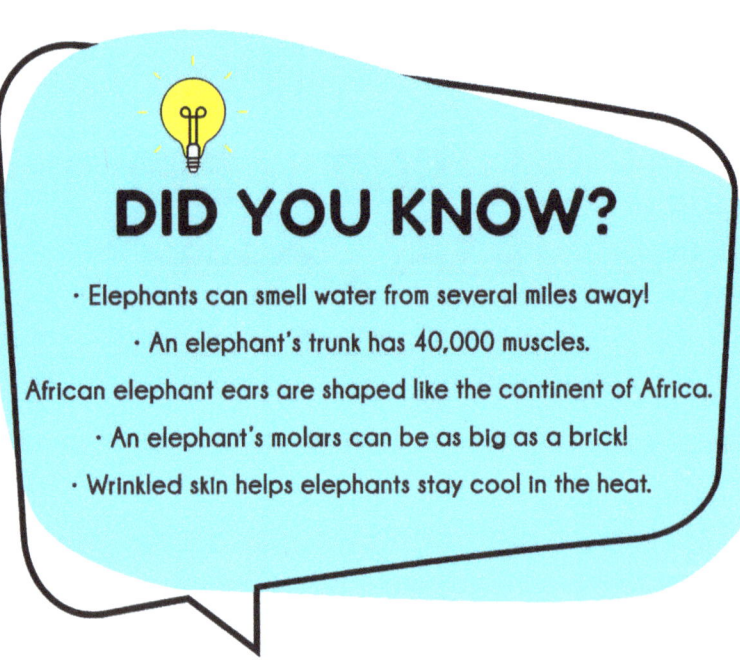

DID YOU KNOW?
- Elephants can smell water from several miles away!
- An elephant's trunk has 40,000 muscles.
- African elephant ears are shaped like the continent of Africa.
- An elephant's molars can be as big as a brick!
- Wrinkled skin helps elephants stay cool in the heat.

Elephants also have tusks, which are actually long teeth made of ivory. Both male and female African elephants have tusks, but in Asian elephants, usually only males grow them. These tusks are used for digging, gathering food, defending against threats, and sometimes battling other elephants.

Elephants have large, round heads with fan-like ears that help keep them cool. Their thick, wrinkled skin helps retain moisture and protects them from harsh sunlight. Unlike most mammals, elephants have special column-like legs designed to support their massive weight, and their broad, cushioned feet allow them to walk quietly despite their size.

Fun Fact: Elephants are left- or right-trunked, just like humans are left- or right-handed.

Fun Fact: Elephants can remember water sources they haven't visited in decades.

Life in Many Lands

Elephants are incredibly adaptable animals that live in a variety of habitats across Africa and Asia including open savannas, dense forests, and even swampy wetlands. Historically, they roamed even more widely, from the steamy rainforests of central Africa to the cool mountains of China.

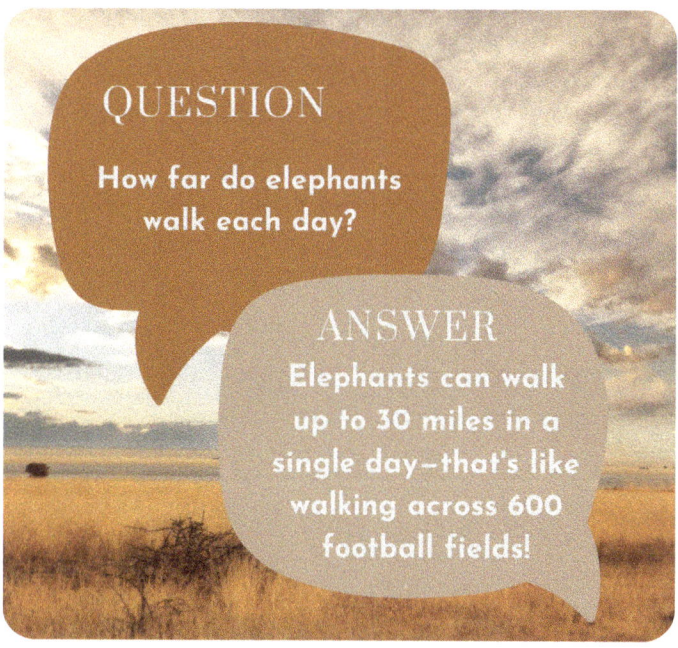

QUESTION How far do elephants walk each day?

ANSWER Elephants can walk up to 30 miles in a single day—that's like walking across 600 football fields!

African savanna elephants prefer open grasslands and scattered woodlands, where they can travel easily in their family groups. African forest elephants make their home in dense rainforests, following ancient pathways through the trees. Asian elephants are the most adaptable, living in different habitats from dense forests to grassy plains and even high mountain areas.

Elephants have adapted to survive in extreme conditions, from scorching heat to heavy monsoon rains. They can handle intense heat over 100°F (38°C) by using their huge ears like fans to cool off and taking mud baths to protect their skin. During dry seasons, they use their trunks and tusks to dig for hidden water sources. Some elephants migrate long distances in search of food and water, following seasonal rains that bring fresh vegetation.

Believe it or not, elephants are surprisingly graceful for their size! They can climb steep mountain trails, wade through deep rivers, and even swim across lakes using their trunks like snorkels. Their large, padded feet help them move quietly through any terrain, from muddy swamps to rocky hillsides.

Super Survivors: Elephant Adaptations

Elephants have developed several physical adaptations that make them perfectly suited to their diverse habitats.

- **Mighty Trunk**: An elephant's trunk is a combination of its nose and upper lip, packed with over 40,000 muscles! It's a powerful tool used for grabbing food, drinking water, communicating, and even lifting heavy objects.

- **Giant Tusk:** These long, curved teeth help elephants dig for water, strip bark from trees, and defend themselves. In African elephants, both males and females have tusks, while in Asian elephants, usually only males grow them.

- **Built-In Cooling System:** Elephants' large ears help them stay cool. By flapping their ears, they create a breeze and release heat through special blood vessels. African elephants, which live in hotter climates, have larger ears than their Asian relatives.

- **Strong, Pillar-Like Legs:** Elephants have thick, column-like legs built to support their massive weight. These sturdy legs work like pillars of a building, allowing elephants to stand for long periods and travel great distances without getting tired.

- **All-Terrain Feet:** Their wide, round feet work like built-in shock absorbers. These special feet allow them to walk almost silently, prevent them from sinking into mud or sand, and help them move smoothly across different terrains from swamps to deserts.

- **Giant Brain:** Elephants have one of the largest brains of any land animal. They use their intelligence for problem-solving, communication, and remembering distant water sources, which is essential for survival.

- **Tough, Wrinkled Skin:** Their thick, wrinkled skin isn't just for protection—it also holds moisture to keep them cool. Elephants often take mud or dust baths, which act as natural sunscreen and insect repellent.

Thanks to these amazing adaptations, elephants don't just survive—they thrive! And they're not just big—they're also some of the smartest animals in the world.

Fun Fact: Elephants can hear sounds so low that humans can't detect them at all.

Fun Fact: Less than half of what an elephant eats is fully digested—the rest feeds other animals and plants.

What Do Elephants Eat?

Elephants are some of the world's most impressive eaters. These huge herbivores spend approximately 12 to 16 hours daily feeding on grasses, fruits, and bark. They can consume up to 350 pounds (160 kilograms) of food each day.

Elephants eat a wide variety of plants. They use their trunks to grasp tall branches, strip bark from trees, or pluck tender grass from the ground. Their tusks help them peel bark and dig up tasty roots. Depending on the season, they might eat grasses, leaves, tree bark, fruits, or roots.

Elephants have special adaptations for processing all this plant material. Their huge molars (back teeth) help them grind tough plants into digestible pieces. These teeth wear down over time, and amazingly, elephants grow new teeth to replace the worn ones throughout their lives. An elephant will have six different sets of molars during its lifetime!

ELEPHANT MATH

> If an adult elephant eats 300 pounds of food per day:
> - How much does it eat in a week?
> - How many pounds would a family of 5 elephants eat in one day?

ANSWER: 2,100 POUNDS PER WEEK; 1,500 POUNDS PER DAY FOR 5 ELEPHANTS

Elephants are also champion drinkers. A single adult can drink up to 50 gallons (190 liters) of water per day. That's enough to fill a bathtub! They use their trunks like a built-in water hose, sucking up water and squirting it into their mouths.

Since they need so much food, elephants are constantly on the move, following seasonal rains that bring new plant growth. Their feeding habits also shape their environment—by knocking down trees and clearing paths, they help create space for new plants to grow, benefiting other animals in their habitat.

Life in the Herd

Elephants are among the most social animals on Earth, living in close family groups led by experienced females called matriarchs. These family groups usually include mothers, daughters, sisters, and young males, and can contain up to 20 elephants. The oldest and wisest female leads the group, making decisions about where to find food, water, and safe places to rest.

Unlike many other animals, elephant families stick together for life. Adult males (bulls) eventually leave to roam on their own or join groups of other males, but females stay with their birth family forever. Different family groups that are related to each other often meet up and greet each other excitedly with trunk-touching, rumbling sounds, and playful behavior.

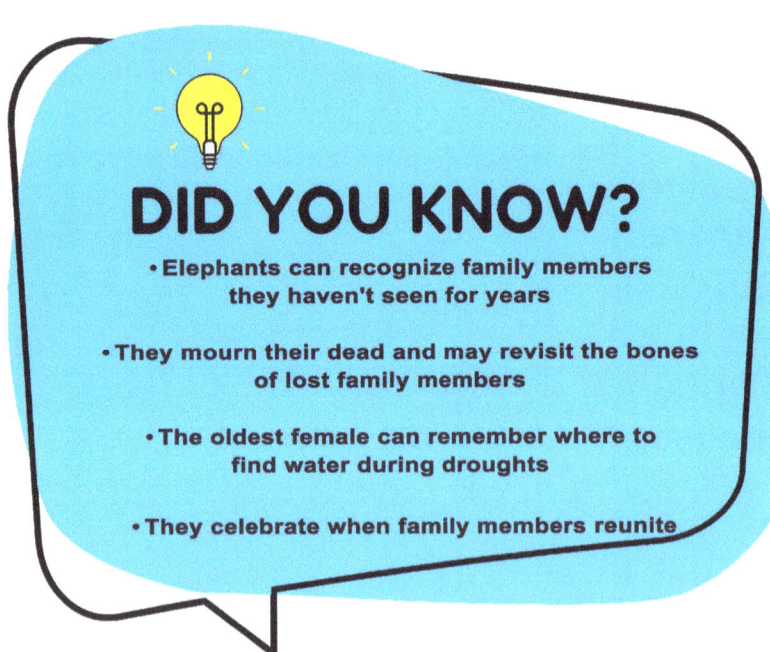

DID YOU KNOW?
- Elephants can recognize family members they haven't seen for years
- They mourn their dead and may revisit the bones of lost family members
- The oldest female can remember where to find water during droughts
- They celebrate when family members reunite

Elephants are amazing communicators. They make many different sounds, from loud trumpets to deep rumbles that humans can't hear but can travel for miles through the ground! They also use body language—raising their trunk in greeting, touching each other gently with their trunks, or flapping their ears when excited.

Young elephants love to play by wrestling, chasing, and splashing in water. This play helps them build strength and learn important social skills. When danger is near, the herd works together—forming a protective circle around the calves while the adults stand ready to defend them.

On the Move

Elephants never stay in one place for too long—they're always on the move, searching for food, water, and safe resting spots. Their movements follow seasonal patterns, often linked to rainfall and the availability of fresh vegetation.

These journeys aren't random—elephants remember traditional migration routes that have been passed down for generations. In dry seasons, they travel toward rivers, lakes, or underground water sources. When the rains return, they spread out to feast on the new growth of grass, leaves, and fruits.

Elephants typically travel 6 to 12 miles (10 to 20 kilometer) per day. However, in search of resources, they can cover distances up to 112 miles (180 kilometers) in a day under certain conditions.

Elephants also leave signs of their presence for others to follow. They create well-worn trails through forests and grasslands, break branches to mark paths, and dig up dry riverbeds in search of water. They communicate their movements through deep rumbles and scent signals, helping herds stay connected even when spread out.

While some elephant populations still migrate naturally, others are limited by human development, such as farms, roads, and fences. Conservation efforts are working to protect elephant corridors—safe pathways that allow them to continue their ancient migrations.

Fun Fact: Elephants often follow the same travel routes year after year, creating paths used for generations.

A Day in the Life

Elephants are active for most of the day and night, spending up to 16 hours a day eating! Since they need to consume hundreds of pounds of food, they are constantly on the move, searching for fresh vegetation.

A typical day for an elephant begins at dawn, when the herd sets out to find food and water. They use their trunks to pull up grass, strip leaves from trees, and dig for roots. During the morning, they cover long distances, walking steadily toward feeding and watering areas.

During the hottest part of the day, especially in summer, elephants seek shade under large trees or cool off in rivers and water holes. They love taking mud baths, coating their skin with mud that protects them from the sun and biting insects—nature's sunscreen and bug repellent! During these rest periods, elephants might take short naps while standing up or lying down, though they always keep some family members alert for danger.

As the day cools in late afternoon, elephants become active again, feeding and often traveling to water sources. Evenings are social times when family members interact, play, and communicate with rumbles and gentle trunk touches. At night, most elephants sleep for a few hours, either standing or lying down, with adults taking turns staying alert to protect the herd.

HOW TO SPOT ELEPHANT MOODS

- Happy: Ears spread wide, trunk swinging, sometimes "purring" sounds
- Curious: Trunk extended forward, ears forward, head raised
- Alarmed: Ears spread out stiffly, trunk raised to smell danger
- Playful: Trunk curled upward, running in short bursts, head shaking
- Aggressive: Ears folded back, trunk tucked in, head held high

Fun Fact: Elephants comfort each other by touching trunks or leaning together.

Mating and Birth

Elephants have a unique and complex mating process. Unlike seasonal breeders, elephants can mate at any time of year, though births often coincide with periods of abundant food and water.

When a female elephant, called a cow, is ready to mate, she signals her availability through scent and behavior. Male elephants, known as bulls, compete for the chance to mate, especially when they enter a state called musth—a period of heightened hormones that makes them more aggressive and dominant. Bulls in musth may fight by pushing, tusking, and wrestling to establish their strength. The strongest bulls usually get the opportunity to mate.

After mating, the female goes through an extraordinarily long pregnancy—about 22 months, the longest of any land animal! She typically gives birth to one calf, though twins are rare. Newborn elephant calves weigh about 200 to 300 pounds (90 to 136 kg) and can stand and walk within hours of birth.

Baby elephants are highly dependent on their mothers and stay close for protection and nourishment. The entire herd helps care for the calf, with older females—called allomothers (helper mothers)—playing a big role in babysitting and teaching.

DID YOU KNOW?

- Elephant mothers and daughters stay together for life
- Elephant calves suck their trunks like human babies suck their thumbs
- Calves drink 3 gallons of milk every day
- Male elephants don't help raise their young

A mother elephant usually gives birth every 4 to 5 years, ensuring she has enough time to care for each calf. The strong bonds within the herd help ensure the survival of young elephants, who spend several years learning from their family before becoming independent.

Growing Up Elephant

Elephant calves are born into a world of constant learning and play. From the moment they stand on their wobbly legs, they begin exploring their surroundings, using their trunks to touch, smell, and interact with everything around them.

At first, baby elephants don't quite know how to use their trunks—it wobbles, flops, and even gets in the way. It takes months of practice before they can skillfully grab food, drink water, or playfully toss dirt onto their backs!

Young elephants are full of energy and love to chase, wrestle, and splash in water. These playful activities aren't just for fun—they help calves develop balance, strength, and important social skills. Play also teaches them how to interact with the herd and prepares young males for the competitive life they will face as adults.

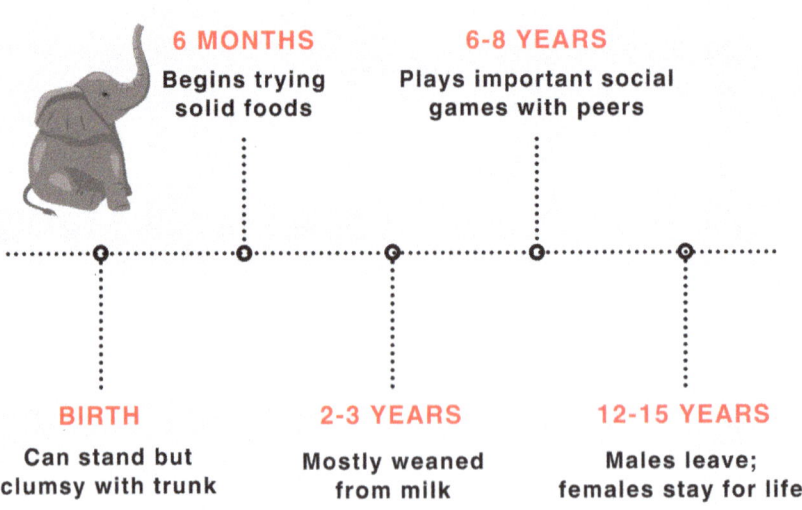

Young elephants don't just learn from mom—the entire family helps raise them. Older sisters, aunts, and grandmothers all take turns watching over the youngsters. These "babysitters" provide protection and teach important social skills. As they grow, calves watch and learn from older elephants. They imitate the way adults break branches, dig for water, and even comfort each other. Young elephants learn by watching adults. This helps them develop skills they'll need to survive.

Male elephants eventually leave their birth families. Between 12-15 years old, young males gradually spend more time at the edge of the herd before joining groups of other males or living alone. Young females, however, stay with their family forever, eventually helping raise their own younger siblings and cousins.

Fun Fact: Elephants are sometimes called "ecosystem engineers" because they shape the land around them.

Elephants and Their Ecosystem

Elephants are vital to their ecosystems in several important ways:

- **Forest and Grassland Management** – Elephants act as natural landscapers, clearing pathways through dense vegetation and opening up areas for new plant growth. Their feeding habits prevent certain plants from overgrowing, helping maintain **biodiversity**.

- **Creating Water Sources** – During dry seasons, elephants use their powerful tusks and trunks to dig deep into dry riverbeds, creating watering holes that benefit not just their herd but also many other animals.

- **Seed Dispersal Experts** – Elephants eat a wide variety of fruits and plants, and their droppings are full of seeds that they spread across vast distances. Some tree species depend entirely on elephants for seed dispersal, making them essential for forest regeneration.

- **Path Creation** – As elephants move through forests and grasslands, they create trails that become wildlife highways used by many other species. These paths connect important resources and help maintain movement corridors through dense vegetation.

- **Supporting Other Species** – Elephants share a close relationship with other wildlife. Birds often pick insects off their backs, and dung beetles rely on elephant droppings to feed and lay their eggs. Their presence supports many species, from tiny insects to large predators.

- **Indicator Species** – Elephant populations reflect the overall health of their ecosystems. Their presence or absence can indicate environmental changes, making them valuable for conservation monitoring.

- **Conservation Icons** – As a keystone species, elephant populations reflect the health of their habitats. Protecting elephants means preserving entire ecosystems, ensuring the survival of countless other species that depend on the same environment.

Elephants don't just survive in their habitats—they shape and sustain them, making them one of the most vital species in the animal kingdom.

Natural Predators

Thanks to their massive size and strong herds, adult elephants have almost no natural predators. However, young elephants, sick individuals, or those separated from the herd can become targets for large carnivores.

- **Lions and Tigers** – In Africa, lions are the main predators of elephants, but they usually only attack calves or weak individuals. In Asia, tigers may also target young elephants, especially those that wander too far from the herd.

- **Crocodiles** – In some regions, large crocodiles have been known to attack young elephants when they come to drink at rivers or watering holes.

- **Hyenas and Wild Dogs** – While they are not a major threat to healthy elephants, packs of spotted hyenas or African wild dogs may try to take down a vulnerable calf if they find one alone.

Despite these threats, elephants are well-equipped to defend themselves. Their size, strength, and sharp tusks make them formidable opponents. When danger approaches, the herd forms a protective circle around the young, with adults facing outward to confront any threat.

Elephants' intelligence and memory also help them avoid danger. They remember safe locations and dangerous areas, and matriarchs teach younger elephants about these threats. Their excellent hearing and sense of smell allow them to detect predators from great distances, giving them time to react and protect the herd.

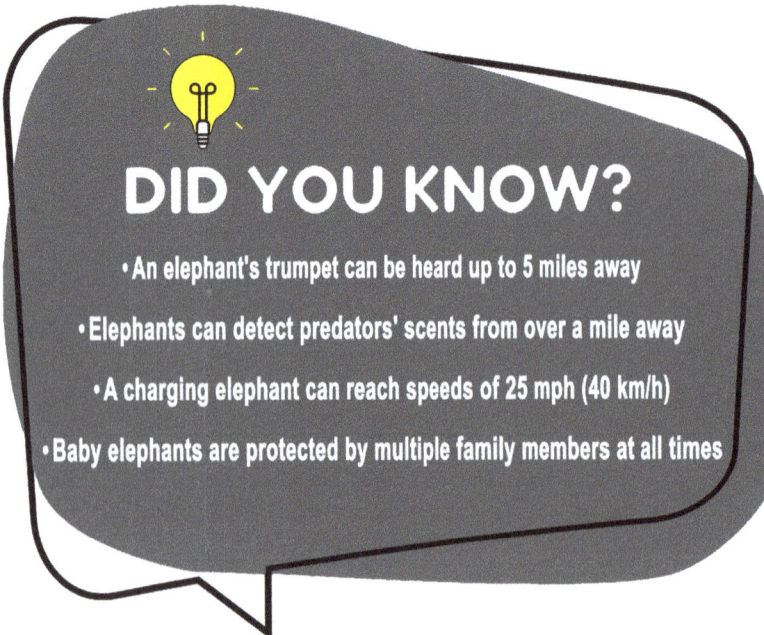

DID YOU KNOW?
- An elephant's trumpet can be heard up to 5 miles away
- Elephants can detect predators' scents from over a mile away
- A charging elephant can reach speeds of 25 mph (40 km/h)
- Baby elephants are protected by multiple family members at all times

Today, the relationship between elephants and natural predators has changed in many places. As human activities have reduced predator populations, many elephants now live in protected areas where large predator encounters are less common. However, in some regions, these natural interactions still occur, helping maintain the delicate balance of their ecosystems.

Fun Fact: Adult elephants can scare predators away just by charging and flapping their ears.

Fun Fact: Protecting elephants also helps protect hundreds of other species that share their habitat.

Challenges and Threats

Aside from natural predators, elephants face several serious threats, most of which are related to human activities:

- **Habitat Loss** – As forests and grasslands are cleared for farms, roads, and cities, elephants are losing the vast spaces they need to roam, find food, and migrate. With fewer wild areas left, elephants are forced into smaller, often fragmented habitats.

- **Poaching and Illegal Wildlife Trade** – One of the biggest threats to elephants is poaching for ivory. Despite international bans on ivory trade, elephants are still killed for their tusks, which are illegally sold for profit. This has led to devastating population declines, especially among African elephants.

- **Human-Wildlife Conflict** – As elephants search for food, they sometimes wander into farmland, damaging crops and property. In some cases, farmers see them as a threat, leading to conflicts that can harm both elephants and people.

- **Climate Change** – Changing weather patterns, including more frequent droughts, can make it harder for elephants to find water and food. Rising temperatures also dry up important watering holes, forcing elephants to travel longer distances to survive.

- **Disease** – Elephants can get sick from different diseases. One dangerous illness that affects baby elephants is called elephant herpes virus. As elephant habitats shrink, the risk of disease spreading between herds increases.

Conservation and Solutions

To protect elephants, conservationists are working on creating wildlife corridors, fighting against illegal poaching, reducing human-elephant conflicts, and restoring lost habitats. Conservation efforts also focus on anti-poaching patrols, elephant sanctuaries, and education programs to promote coexistence between elephants and humans.

By protecting elephants, we are also preserving the ecosystems they shape and ensuring future generations can witness these incredible giants in the wild.

Life Span and Population

Elephants are some of the longest-living land animals—wild elephants typically live between 50 to 70 years, and some even reach 80! Elephants in protected areas and sanctuaries tend to live longer because they have access to veterinary care and are shielded from poaching and other threats.

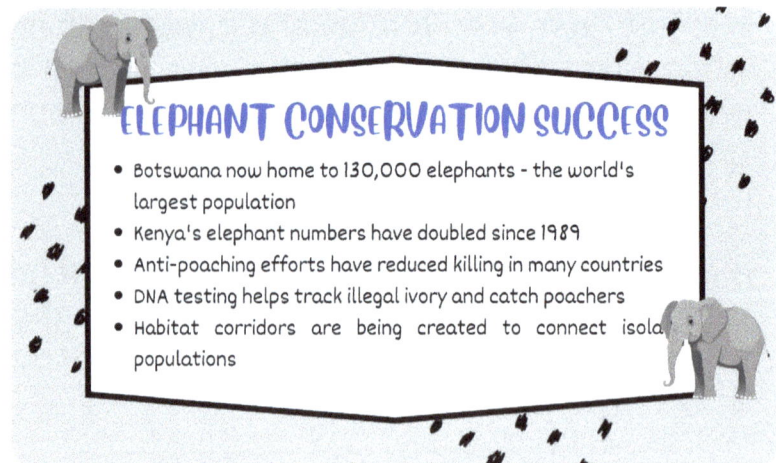

Elephants were once widespread across Africa and Asia, but their numbers have declined dramatically due to habitat loss and poaching. Today, there are two main types of elephants:

- **African Elephants** – Estimated 415,000 remain in the wild.
- **Asian Elephants** – Fewer than 50,000 remain, making them endangered.

African elephants live in national parks and reserves across countries like Botswana, Kenya, and South Africa. Some of the largest wild populations are found in places like the Okavango Delta in Botswana and Amboseli National Park in Kenya.

Asian elephants have a smaller range, mostly in India, Sri Lanka, Thailand, and Myanmar. Unlike their African relatives, many Asian elephants live in forested areas, making them harder to count accurately.

While conservation efforts have helped protect some elephant populations, they still face major threats. Many organizations work to reduce poaching, create wildlife corridors, and promote peaceful coexistence between humans and elephants. Protecting these gentle giants is essential—not just for their survival but for the health of the ecosystems they help maintain.

Fun Fact: Some elephant populations are increasing thanks to conservation efforts.

Future for Elephants

Elephants are among the most majestic and intelligent animals on Earth. Throughout this book, we've discovered what makes elephants some of the planet's most extraordinary creatures. From their incredible family bonds to their critical role in ecosystems, elephants show us how the natural world is connected in remarkable ways.

Elephants are full of surprises. In addition to being the largest land animals, they are also among the most gentle and intelligent. They can remember migration routes for decades, communicate across miles using sounds too low for human ears, and form emotional bonds that last a lifetime. Their remarkable trunks—with more muscles than the entire human body—allow them to perform tasks requiring both power and delicate precision.

Even though elephants are strong, they face many challenges today. They're losing their homes as forests are cut down, and some are still hunted for their tusks. When we protect elephants, we also protect the forests, grasslands, and water sources that many other animals need to survive.

Conservation efforts around the world have already made a difference. In some regions, elephant populations are stabilizing or even growing, proving that when people come together to protect wildlife, real change is possible. Efforts like wildlife corridors, anti-poaching patrols, and habitat restoration offer hope for a future where elephants can continue to roam freely.

Seeing elephants in the wild is a powerful reminder of the world we share with them—a world where every species plays a part in maintaining nature's delicate balance. By protecting elephants today, we ensure that future generations can experience the awe and wonder of these magnificent creatures.

The story of elephant conservation is far from over, but with continued dedication, we can help secure a future where elephants not only survive but thrive in the wild for generations to come.

Test Your Elephant Knowledge!

Think you remember everything about these gentle giants? Test yourself with these questions!

🐘 1. What is the scientific family name for elephants?
A) Pachydermia B) Elephantidae C) Proboscidea D) Mammalidae

🐘 2. True or False: Both male and female African elephants grow tusks.

🐘 3. How much food can an adult elephant eat in a single day?
A) 50 pounds B) 150 pounds C) Up to 350 pounds D) 500 pounds

🐘 4. What is the leader of an elephant herd called?
A) Alpha B) Queen C) Matriarch D) Chief

🐘 5. How long is an elephant's pregnancy?
A) 9 months B) 12 months C) 18 months D) 22 months

🐘 6. How many muscles are in an elephant's trunk?
A) 1,000 B) 10,000 C) 40,000 D) 100,000

🐘 7. What do elephants use their large ears for?
A) Better hearing B) Cooling off C) Communication D) All of the above

🐘 8. How many sets of molars will an elephant have during its lifetime?
A) 2 B) 4 C) 6 D) 8

🐘 9. Approximately how many African elephants remain in the wild today?
A) 50,000 B) 150,000 C) 415,000 D) 1 million

🐘 10. What term describes an important animal that many other plants and animals depend on?
A) Apex predator B) Keystone species C) Herbivore D) Ecosystem engineer

Answer Key: 1-B, 2-True, 3-C, 4-C, 5-D, 6-C, 7-D, 8-C, 9-C, 10-B

STEM Challenge: Think Like a Scientist!

Elephants are built for power and survival. Try these hands-on experiments to discover how their amazing adaptations help them thrive!

Trunk Power Challenge

Topic: Anatomy & Engineering

You'll Need:
A flexible straw, a cup of water, small objects (paperclip, cotton ball, penny), timer

What to Do:
1. Use only the straw (no hands!) to pick up different objects by creating suction
2. Time how long it takes to move each object from one spot to another
3. Now try sucking water into the straw and releasing it into a cup
4. Which tasks were easiest? Which were hardest?

What You'll Learn:
An elephant's trunk works like a powerful combination of a nose and a hand. With over 40,000 muscles, it can lift 700 pounds—yet also pick up a single peanut! Your straw shows how suction and precision work together.

Wrinkly Skin Cooling Test

Topic: Biology & Heat Transfer

You'll Need:
Two paper towels, water, a sunny window or warm lamp, timer

What to Do:
1. Wet both paper towels equally
2. Lay one flat and smooth
3. Scrunch the other into deep wrinkles and folds
4. Place both in the warm spot and check every 10 minutes
5. Which one stays damp longer?

What You'll Learn:
Elephant skin has deep wrinkles that trap moisture and mud, keeping them cool in hot climates. The wrinkled towel holds water in its folds—just like elephant skin acts as a natural cooling system!

Word Search

```
C V E C O S Y S T E M L O E W
C O V N O I T A L U P O P H E
S O N L I B U L L S W S A C Z
K A W S Y N L V B M I L U R K
S Z H S E F G L N T V S A A O
U S O E P R W S S X S I N I T
T U T T R E V W C N S G O R E
P K C R X B S A O A Y G I T R
A Z F W U E I I T Q P E T A R
F X D E V N T V I I N V A M I
R Q O L P A K Q O O O K R Q T
I I A E T N U B T R X N G D O
C C X P P Q S S K U E J I W R
A P A H D C Y R U T I J M P Y
O D S A U E I A N N A V A S W
A G U N K X S D R E H S W I R
V F N T H A B I T A T O Z G J
J M R S S P R E D A T O R S W
```

Adaptations	Ecosystem	Migration
Africa	Elephants	Population
Asia	Habitat	Predators
Bulls	Herbivore	Savanna
Calves	Herds	Territory
Conservation	Keystone	Trunk
Cows	Matriarch	Tusks

Glossary

adaptations – special body parts or behaviors that help animals survive in their environment

biodiversity – the variety of different types of plants and animals living in an area

bulls – adult male elephants

calves – baby elephants

cows – adult female elephants

ecosystem – a community of living things and their environment, and how they interact with each other

endangered – at serious risk of dying out completely

habitat – the natural home or environment where a plant or animal lives

herbivores – animals that eat only plants

herd – a group of elephants that live and travel together

ivory – the hard, white material that elephant tusks are made of

keystone species – an important animal that many other plants and animals depend on for survival

matriarch – the oldest and wisest female who leads an elephant herd

migration – when animals travel long distances to find food, water, or better weather as seasons change

molars – large, flat back teeth used for grinding food

monsoon – a season of heavy rains and strong winds that comes at the same time each year

musth – a period when male elephants have high hormones and become more aggressive

poaching – illegally hunting and killing protected animals

savanna – a grassland ecosystem with scattered trees, found in tropical regions

territory – an area that an animal considers its home and may defend from others

tusks – long teeth made of ivory that elephants use for digging, gathering food, and defense

Resources and References

Want to learn more about elephants? Check out these trusted books, websites, and organizations that explore wildlife, science, and conservation.

Books

Elephants by Laura Marsh (National Geographic Kids) — Perfect for young readers who want fun facts and stunning photos.

The Elephant Scientist by Caitlin O'Connell and Donna M. Jackson (Houghton Mifflin) — Follow a real scientist studying elephant communication.

Elephant Talk: The Surprising Science of Elephant Communication by Ann Downer (Twenty-First Century Books) — Discover how elephants "talk" to each other.

Websites

National Geographic Kids – Elephant Facts
kids.nationalgeographic.com/animals/mammals/facts/african-elephant
Fun facts, videos, and photos perfect for young elephant fans.

World Wildlife Fund (WWF) – Elephant Conservation
worldwildlife.org/species/elephant
Learn about global efforts to protect elephants and their habitats.

African Wildlife Foundation
awf.org/wildlife-conservation/elephant
Explore programs protecting elephants across Africa.

San Diego Zoo Wildlife Alliance – Elephants
animals.sandiegozoo.org/animals/elephant
Detailed information, videos, and conservation stories.

For Young Scientists

Elephant Voices
elephantvoices.org
Hear real elephant sounds and learn how scientists decode their communication.

Save the Elephants
savetheelephants.org
Discover cutting-edge research on elephant behavior and tracking.

Keep Exploring!

If you enjoyed learning about elephants, explore other titles in the This Incredible Planet series to discover more amazing animals—from sea turtles to penguins to lions—and the habitats they call home.

Index

A
adaptations, 12
African elephants, 7, 11, 32
allo-mothers, 23
Asian elephants, 7, 11, 32

B
birth, 23
body language, 16
brain, 12

C
calves, 16, 23, 24
challenges, 31, 35
climate change, 31
communication, 16
conservation, 18, 27, 31, 32, 35
crocodiles, 28

D
daily life, 20
diet, 15
disease, 31

E
ears, 8, 11, 12
eating, 20
ecosystems, 26, 27
environment, 7, 11

F
family groups, 16, 23, 24
feet, 12
females, 16, 23, 24
food sources, 15

H
habitat, 7, 11
habitat loss, 31
herds, 16
human conflict, 31
hyenas, 28

I
indicator species, 27
intelligence, 7, 28
ivory, 31

K
keystone species, 27

L
legs, 12
life span, 32
lions, 28

M
males, 16, 23, 24
mating, 23
matriarchs, 16, 28
memory, 10, 12, 28
migration, 18
molars, 15
moods, 20
mud baths, 20

P
parenting, 23
physical adaptations, 12
physical appearance, 8
poaching, 31
population, 32
predators, 28
pregnancy, 23

S
seasons, 18
seed dispersal, 27
senses, 8, 13, 28
size, 8
skin, 7, 8, 12
sleeping, 20
social behavior, 7, 16, 20

T
teeth, 15
threats, 31
tigers, 28
trails, 27
trunk, 6, 8, 9, 11, 12, 15, 24
tusks, 8, 11, 12, 15, 28

W
water, 15
water sources, 27
weight, 8
wild dogs, 28

www.ingramcontent.com/pod-product-compliance
Lightning Source LLC
Chambersburg PA
CBHW040224040426
42333CB00051B/3435